Say What You See

Animals

Rebecca Rissman

Raintree

Raintree is an imprint of Capstone Global Library Limited, a company incorporated in England and Wales having its registered office at 7 Pilgrim Street, London, EC4V 6LB – Registered company number: 6695582

www.raintreepublishers.co.uk
myorders@raintreepublishers.co.uk

Text © Capstone Global Library Limited 2013
First published in hardback in 2013
Paperback edition first published in 2014
The moral rights of the proprietor have been asserted.

Edited by Rebecca Rissman, Daniel Nunn, and Catherine Veitch
Designed by Philippa Jenkins
Picture research by Ruth Blair
Production by Victoria Fitzgerald
Originated by Capstone Global Library
Printed and bound in China

ISBN 978 1 406 25140 1 (hardback)
16 15 14 13 12
10 9 8 7 6 5 4 3 2 1

ISBN 978 1 406 25145 6 (paperback)
16 15 14 13 14
10 9 8 7 6 5 4 3 2 1

British Library Cataloguing in Publication Data
Rissman, Rebecca.
Animals. -- (Say What You See!)
590-dc23
A full catalogue record for this book is available from the British Library.

Acknowledgements
We would like to thank the following for permission to reproduce photographs: Shutterstock pp. title page (© Eric Isselée), 4 (© Michael Wick), 5 (© Nejron Photo, © Utekhina Anna, © Anatema), 6 (© Zachary Garber), 7 (© Vera Kailova, © Utekhina Anna, © Pichugin Dmitry), 8 (© Tomas Sereda, © Christian Musat), 9 (© Ervin Monn, © Dudarev Mikhail), 10 (© Jarek Joepera, © FedericoPhotos), 11 (© Barry Blackburn, © Matt Jeppson), 12 (© Krzysztof Odziomek, © Steve Noakes), 13 (© Pichugin Dmitry, © Eric Gevaert), 14 (© intoit), 15 (© Bo Valentino), 16 (© Geanina Bechea, © Ervin Monn), 17 (© Zadiraka Evgenii), 18 (© Cheryl Ann Quigley), 19 (© Johan Swanepoel, © Wild At Art, © Ronnie Howard), 20 (© Daniel Alvarez, © Stefanie van der Vinden), 21 (© Ronald van der Beek), 22 (© siamionau pavel).

Cover photograph of a yellow-eyed cat reproduced with permission of Shutterstock (© Stankevich).

Every effort has been made to contact copyright holders of material reproduced in this book. Any omissions will be rectified in subsequent printings if notice is given to the publisher.

Contents

Animals have a lot to say....... 4

Humans have a lot
to say, too 22

Can you find these
things in the book?............. 23

Index 24

Animals have a lot to say... What are they saying?

Hoo, hoo

MOO!

6

Purr, purr

Meow!

Hiss

"Cluck cluck"

Cockadoodle doo!

Hee haw! Hee haw!

Quack, quack!

Roar!

Eee eee eee ooooh ooh!

21

Humans have a lot to say, too.

Hello, there!

Can you find these things in the book? Look back... and say what you see!

kitten

lion

snake

duck

Index

bird 4, 8, 9, 16, 17
cat 7
chicken 8
chimpanzee 21
cockerel 8
cow 6
dog 5
dolphin 12
donkey 14
duck 16
goose 17
horse 10
human 22

hyena 20
kitten 7
lamb 13
lion 18, 19
owl 4
parrot 9
pigeon 17
pony 10
puppy 5
sheep 13
snake 11
toad 15
wolf 19